Make Your Own Slide Guitar

The Dr Jazz Workshop Manual

Clinical Press Ltd

Clinical Press Ltd Publishers, Bristol, United Kingdom

© *Paul R Goddard,* **2023**

The right of Paul R Goddard to be identified as the author and artist of this work has been asserted by him in accordance with the Copyright, Designs and Patents Act 1988.

All rights reserved. No part of this publication may be reproduced, stored in a retrieval system, or transmitted in any form or by any means, electronic, mechanical, photocopying, recording or otherwise, without prior permission from the copyright owner.

While the advice and information in this book is believed to be true and accurate at the time of going to press, neither the author, the editor, nor the publisher can accept legal responsibility for any errors or omissions that may be made. The publisher makes no warranty, express or implied, with respect to the material contained herein.

First published in the UK 2023

A catalogue record for this book is available from the British Library
ISBN: **978-1-85457-122-9** *Make your own slide guitar*

Published by:
Clinical Press Ltd. Redland Green Farm, Redland, Bristol, BS6 7HF

Chapter 1

The Dr Jazz Slide Guitar

Simple schematic of a cigar box slide guitar

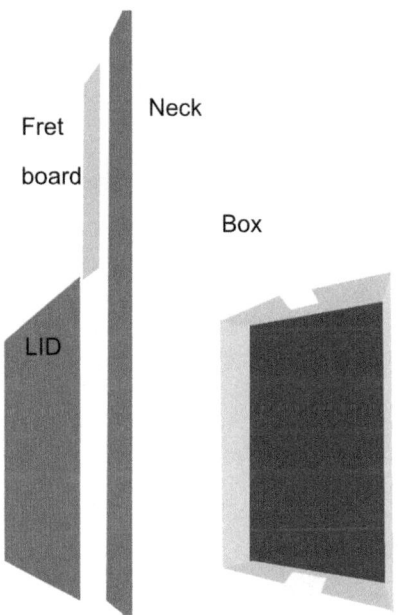

The neck is glued to the lid. A gap is cut in the box sides. The lid is reattached using hinges (or screws).

In the example detailed in this book the lid is hinged and a gap is cut in both the head end and tail end of the box.

Golden Rule: A slide guitar does not have to be perfect. Don't let the perfect be the enemy of the good.

What is needed

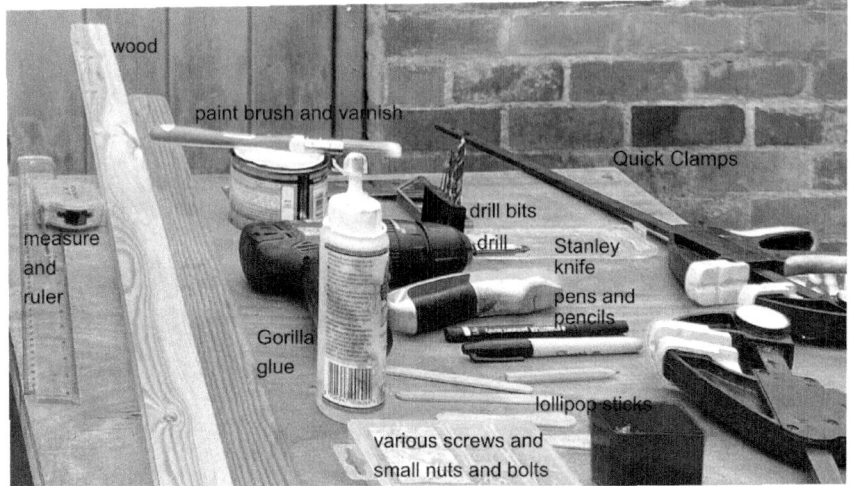

Required tools include: *Drill (mains, battery or mechanical), drill bits, measure, ruler, paint brush and varnish, Stanley knife, chisel (1 cm), clamps, lollipop sticks, screws, bolts, nuts, hammer, clamps, sandpaper, hand saw, screwdrivers, 2 adjustable spanners, round rasp or file, Gorilla glue (clear).*

Materials for this slide guitar:
- *A typical cigar box (right)*
- *Pickups (piezo-electric) (below)*

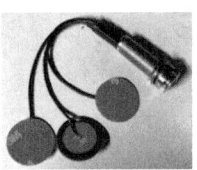

- *3 Tuning pegs (machine heads)*

- *Wood for the neck and fretboard,*
- *Metal plate for tail piece (Meccano)*

Cigar boxes can be bought online from ebay for as little as £3 to £4. It is probably worth buying two or three so that you can choose between them and even practice on the one you don't like! Alternatively you may be able to cadge a box or two from friends.

Pieces of wood,
1 piece : 1 metre of planed 50 mm by 25mm (2" by 1") Finish 20.5mm x 44mm. (About £4 from B and Q)
1 piece: flat pine moulding, rounded front edges, 1 metre length, 40 mm width, 5mm depth: about £5
Such pieces are common and can often be found in skips for free.

Pickups
These are available new from ebay. They are nearly all made in China. For this guitar we are using piezo-electric pickups.

Machine Heads
Similarly new machine heads (tuning pegs) are also available online from China.I have occasionally found broken guitars with pickups in the garbage and skips.

Tail piece: Possible metal pieces include hinges, striker plates and brackets. For this guitar a small Meccano double angle strip will be used (5 holes total, 3 in the middle, one at each end.)

Bolts
Suitable nuts and bolts for use as guitar bridges can be purchased cheaply from hardware or DIY or discount stores.

Warning: Varnish You can use a low odour, water-based varnish but it will take many coats to build up a suitable shine. If you use naphtha-based varnish the finish is better but the varnish is **toxic** and must be done outside not indoors. Wear protective gloves, mask and clothing.

Dimensions

The cigar box we are working on in this book measured 190mm by 160mm by 40mm. Any small wooden box can be used ! The neck measured 820mm in total. Scale length 640mm, Fretboard 550mm, machine head plate (part of the neck in this design) 60mm.

Chapter 2

Step 1: Preparing the box

2.0 Give the chosen cigar box and the wood for the neck a varnish using a paintbrush. You will either have to wait 24 hours while it dries (naphtha-based) or build up with repeated low odour coatings.

2.1 Taking the already varnished box secure it in the workbench and drill small holes for the doll's house 'hook and eye' catch . The catches are difficult to find in DIY or hardware stores and often not stocked but can easily be purchased online.

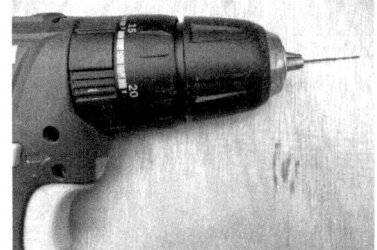

This particular box had no catch but was well hinged so the hook and eye were added. Many boxes will require a new hinge also.

Golden Rule: Always secure the object you are working on. Most accidents occur when using tools and can be avoided by carefully securing the object. Also: use safety goggles and gloves.

2.2. Measure the width of the box from front to back.

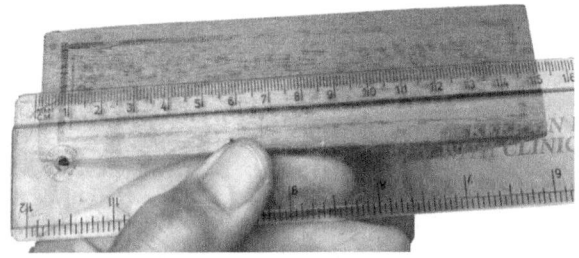

2.3. The width of the long piece of wood should now be measured

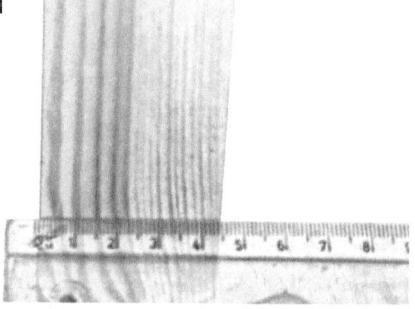

It will be about 44mm for planed wood that was originally 50 mm by 25mm (2" by 1") before planing.

2.4. Find the centre spot of the width of the box.

2.5. Measure half the width of the neck out from the centre spot and drop down a line using a ball point pen or sharp pencil and a set square.

Using a set square draw a line to connect the two marked lines. You now have your cut lines.

2.6. Secure the box on the workbench and cut down the marked lines using a hacksaw or equivalent. Remove the middle piece using either a Stanley knife or hammer and chisel.

Secure the box and cut down the vertical mark

The piece at the head end has been removed and the tail end vertical cuts have been done. The piece is then removed using a chisel or Stanley knife. For safety I work the knife <u>away</u> from me. Keep the pieces as they may be used later.

2.7. Making a hole for the pickup socket.

The hole for the pickup socket is usually at the tail end of the guitar. Work out where the piezo electric pads will be placed and make sure that there is sufficient wire to reach the site you choose for the socket.

Make a small hole first and then enlarge the hole with a larger drill bit. Usually a 10mm drill bit is needed but the walls of this box were too thick for the outer part of the socket thread. Because of the width of the walls in this case a 13mm drill bit was used. If you are in doubt make a hole in a scrap piece of wood that you have first secured well on the bench.

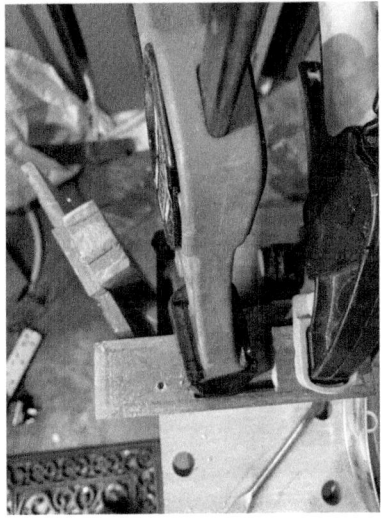

Drill a guide hole first (left)

Then drill the larger hole if needed (right)

2.8. Make some holes for the sound to escape!

This is an acoustic slide guitar so some holes for the sound to escape would be useful!

In order to leave the sound board unaltered the sound holes were made in the wall of the box facing the player. This is the hinge side. You may wish to have the sound holes on the box lid. You can choose.

The box was secured using a kneeling pad on either side of the box. 3mm holes were first drilled followed by enlargement to 6 mm.

Washers were stuck on the holes as decoration.

(You do not have to do this!)

2.9. Mark on the inside of the lid two lines from the top of the cuts. This is where the neck will later be stuck.

2.10. Put the piece of planed 2" by 1" in the cut holes and close the lid. Decide on the length of the neck Measure the required length of neck. (typically about 70 cm but depending on the size of the cigar box).

2.11. Give the box another coat of varnish and leave it for 24 hours. (Or several coats of low odour varnish). Varnish the neck and the fretboard (the flat pine moulding).

<u>Golden Rule</u>:

Wear disposable gloves when gluing or varnishing

Always clean brushes immediately after use.

Chapter 3

Preparing the neck

3.1 Cut the neck to length.

Before varnishing the box at the end of chapter 1 you should have offered up the piece of planed wood that you are using for a neck and decided on a length. This could be anything between 40 cm to 85 cm depending on the size of the cigar box and your own preference regarding the final look of the guitar. We used 82cm (820mm).

Cut the piece to size. (I'm using a floorboard saw!)

Golden Rule: measure 3 times and cut once. Be obsessional about measurement and the task will be more straightforward.

3.2 Mark the position for the machine heads. You can either use the template provided here:-

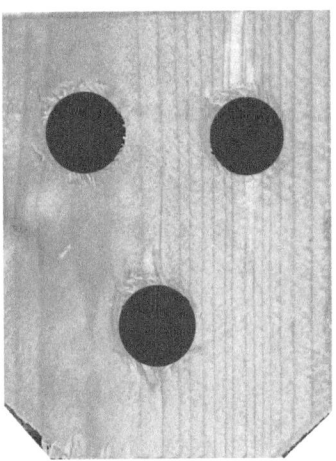

3.2.1 Or offer up the machine heads and judge where they should go.

Offering up the machine heads

The machine heads are placed approximately and positions roughly marked

3.3 Drill guide holes for the machine heads

The neck has been securely attached to the workbench but also a quick gripper has been fastened from side to side as there is otherwise a possibility of the wood splitting when being drilled, especially when creating relatively large holes. The size of drill holes required will depend on your type of machine heads.

3.4 Drill the full-sized holes

3.5 If necessary reduce the depth of the neck at the site of the machine heads

Some machine head posts are too short to go through the depth of the neck so the neck has to be narrowed at the site of the machine heads by cutting off a suitably sized piece. Do this after the holes have been drilled in order to reduce the danger of the wood splitting.

3.6 Try fitting the machine heads temporarily.

Take the machine heads out.

3.7 Sand the newly exposed wood and the back and sides of the neck.

 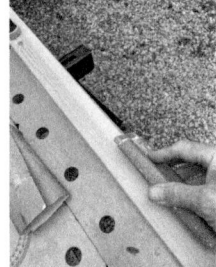

3.8 Tailpiece

A tailpiece is require or the strings will cut through the wood.

Possible metal pieces include hinges, striker plates and brackets. For this guitar a small Meccano double angle strip will be used. These are available very cheaply online or in charity shops

Two lines are marked where the legs of the strip will be positioned.

3.9 Cut down the lines and push the legs into the grooves.

Cut off the corners of the tail of the neck. Drill small holes (2mm diameter) through the three visible holes of the Meccano strip.

The neck is now complete and ready for attaching to the lid.

Chapter 4

Attaching the neck and fretboard

In this chapter the neck and fretboard are attached to the guitar.

4.1 Glue

Golden Rule:

For the purpose of making Dr Jazz guitars I always use "Gorilla Glue Clear" throughout. Because it is a strong, clear, transparent glue it is not a big problem if a tiny extra amount of glue seeps onto adjacent parts. It is very strong and glues nearly everything securely including wood, plastic and metal.

4.2 Instruction 2.9 asked you to mark the inside of the lid.

To do this mark the site of the cut out on the edge of the lid at both ends.

Joining the marks by two lines will show you where to stick the neck. Make sure that sufficient tail sticks out at the end for you to string the guitar without having to open the lid.

The lines marked on the inside of the lid

Diagram showing the neck being glued to the inside of the lid

4.3 The flat pine moulding should already have been varnished at least once (see 2.11). Take the already varnished flat pine moulding or equivalent and offer up to the neck. You can now decide exactly how long the fretboard should be by leaving at least 60mm of neck for the machine heads.

Schematic showing how the fretboard is offered up to the neck.

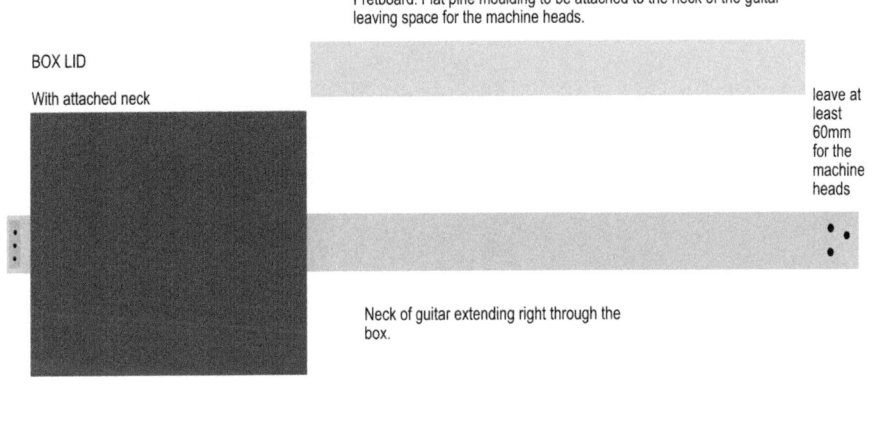

4.4 Mark with a pencil and set square. Cut to length required

4.5 Take a round file and rasp a groove at the machine heads' end of the fretboard.

Round file in hand.

Pine moulding secured on workbench

Groove very near the end of the fretboard

The groove will be the "bed" for a bolt which will later act as the bridge at the machine heads' end of the fretboard.

4.6 Attach the fretboard to the neck using Gorilla glue.

The fretboard has been glued to the neck and clamped. In normal conditions the glue will take two hours to get a firm hold so keep the clamps on for at least that time. Full bonding strength takes 24 hours.

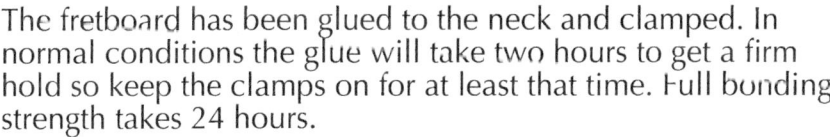

If you have not previously varnished the fretboard pine moulding do it now and leave for 24 hours. You can give other parts of the guitar a coat of varnish at the same time!

Chapter 5

In which we make the bridges and tidy up the guitar

5.1 Making the bridges

The bridges can be made from metal (usually bolts) or wood. This time we are combining the two for the body bridge.

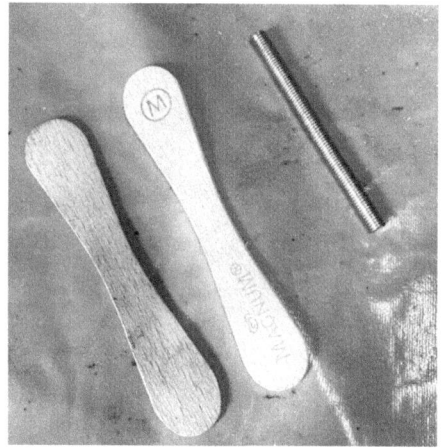

To make the bridge we took two lollipop sticks and a piece of threaded bar.

5.2 The two lollipop sticks are first struck to each other and then the thread is stuck onto the top.

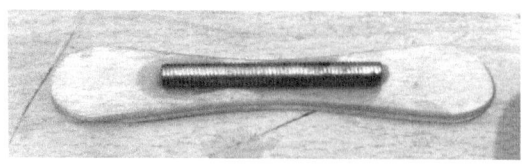

Of course we used Gorilla glue.

If you have no threaded bar you can cut the head off a bolt but that is wasteful.

5.3 The machine heads' end bridge (see 4.5) is simply a bolt. You can stick a nut to the end of the bolt if you wish but this is aesthetically pleasing rather than necessary.

5.4 Tidying up the appearance of the guitar.

We want the guitar to open with the neck attached to the lid. Because the lid is hinged this means either that

- The slot in the box either has to be widened obliquely (as shown above)

- Or the neck needs to be trimmed so that it has a more rounded profile.

- Or a slot has to be cut in the neck.

At the machine heads' end of the box the slot was reshaped to be more oblique. There was also too much of a gap at the back and front of the slot.

5.5 The gap at the back was covered with a piece of lolly stick

5.6 Similarly the gap at the front was filled with the other half of the lolly stick. This also hid the wide gap at the side from the direct gaze.

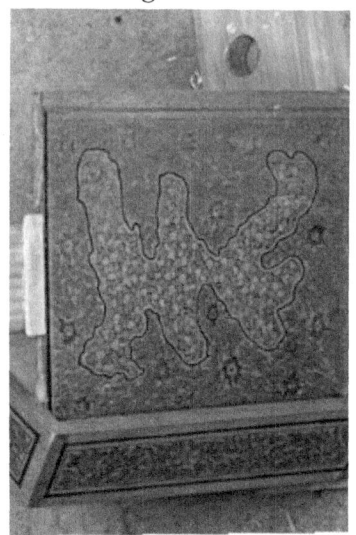

The piece from the box side cut out was pared down and re-fitted at the tail end.

The main parts of the guitar are now in place.
5.7 Sand and varnish the guitar. Leave for 24 hours.

Chapter 6

Marking the fretboard

6.1 First check that the fretboard is thoroughly dry.

6.2 Measure in millimetres from the middle of the machine heads' end bridge groove to the position that you would like to put the box bridge. This is the scale length: the length of the active string. Our scale length was 640 mm.

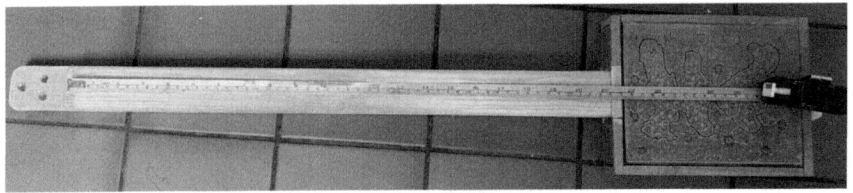

6.3 Look up a fret calculator on the internet

Example: (https://manchesterguitartech.co.uk/fret-and-nut-calculators/fret-calculator/).

Some examples are given at the end of this book in the appendix for people who do not have internet access (page 40). Do not be constrained by these measurements. Your cigar box and neck will not be identical to ours. You are creating a unique artwork!

Enter the length measured in 6.2 into the fret calculator or use the appendix. Put your longest clear plastic ruler on the fretboard.

6.4 Using a permanent felt tip marker, put dots on the fretboard where the fret line should be. I use a Sharpie fine point.

Golden Rule :

The most accurate way to mark your scale is making all measurements from the bridge groove (using the "fret to fret" distance only to confirm your layout). Laying out frets only by measuring fret to fret will compound error.

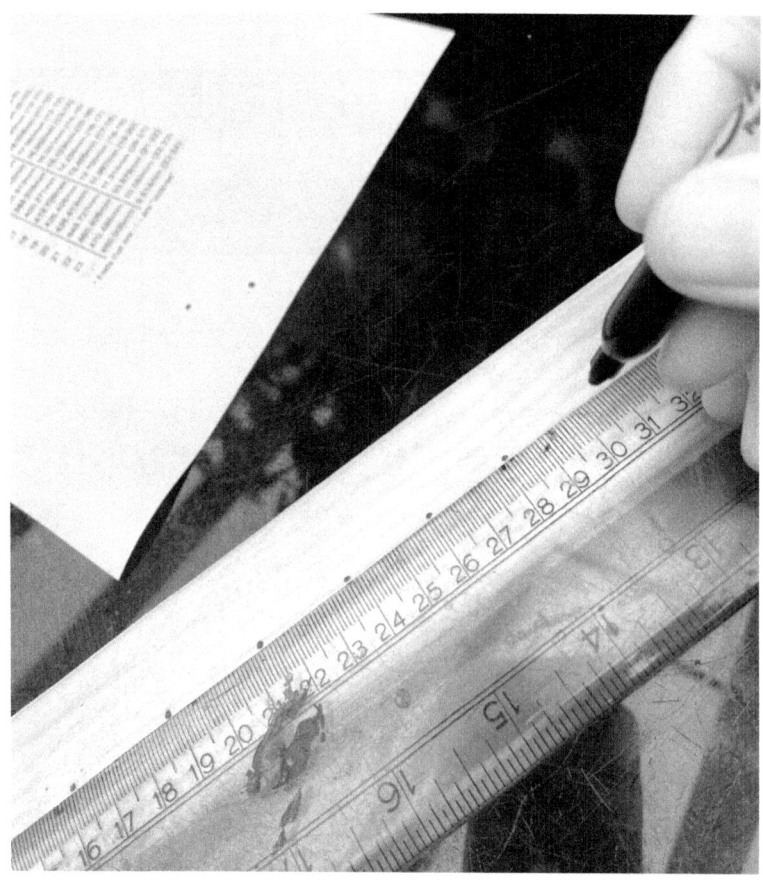

Marking the position for the fret lines.

Note: This is a slide guitar. We will not be using metal tangs.

6.5 Draw the lines using a carpenter's metal set square and a felt tip marker pen.

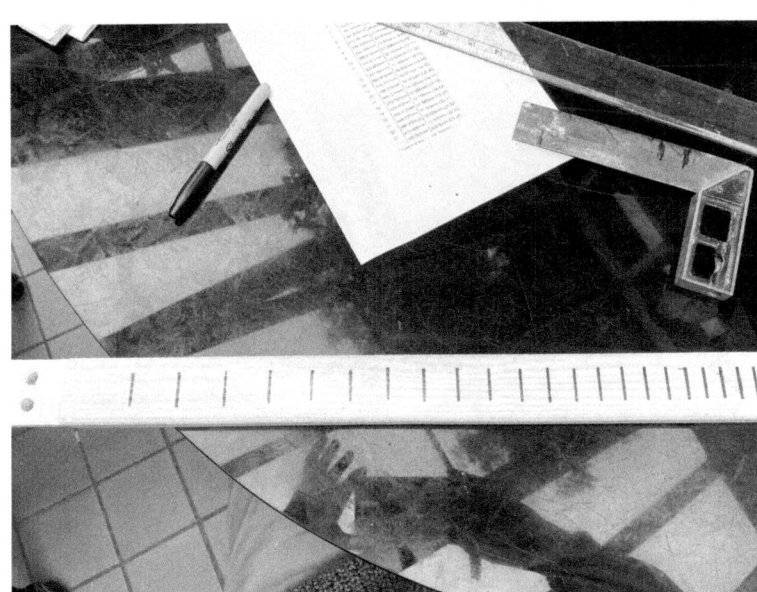

6.6 Draw the fret markers on the fret spaces. Alternatively you can inlay jewels, fancy buttons or whatever. We have kept it simple with this guitar but this is your chance to be fancy.

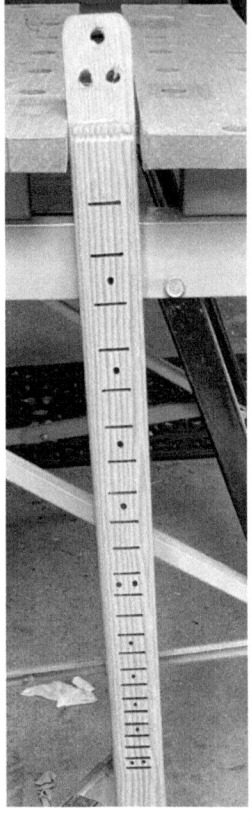

The markers are the round dots in the fret spaces. They are there to help guitarists find their way around the fretboard. As this is a slide guitar they are only approximate positions. For slide guitar they are usually positioned on fret spaces 3,5,7,9,12,15,17,19, 21,24.

12 and 24 have 2 dots each as they are octaves.

6.7 Time to re-varnish. This should be done with non-water soluble varnish as water soluble varnish can smudge the felt tip pen marks.

Golden Rule: If you are worried try the varnish on a scrap piece of wood. Leave to dry then mark a line. Paint over with varnish. Leave for 24 hours.

Chapter 7

Attaching the pickups

7.1 Take the pickups out of the cellophane.

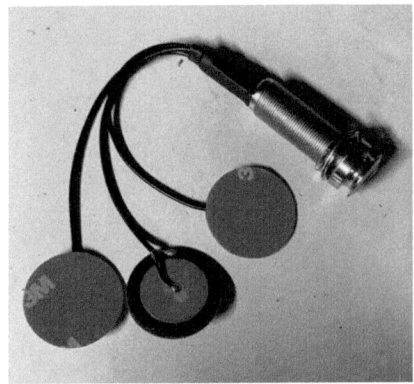

The pickups can be purchased on ebay. The cheapest ones come from China and cost about £7 or less for a 3 transducer pickup set. Search for Acoustic Piezo Contact Microphone Pickup for Guitar

7.2 Push the thread through the hole so that it appears on the other side with sufficient thread to screw on the securing nut.

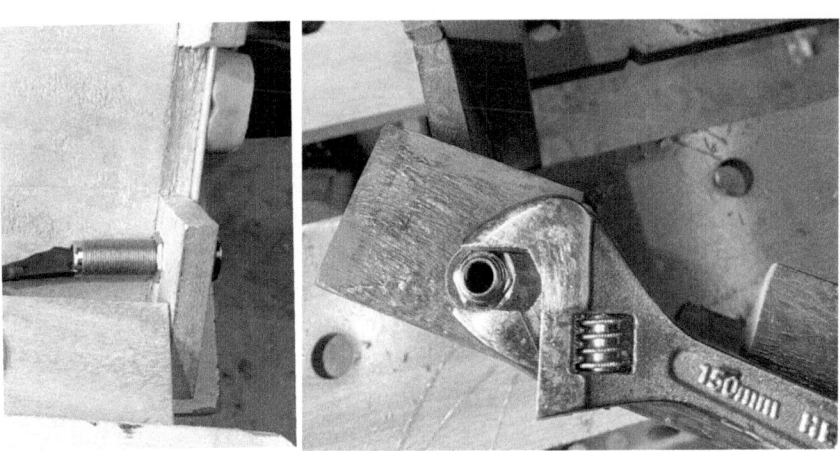

Screw the nut tight using two adjustable spanners: one on the inside nut and one on the outside.

7.2

Screw on the finishing capping nut. This is tightened by hand

7.3 Peel off the plastic layer protecting the sticky surface of the piezo-electric microphones.

The plastic layer is labelled 3M and must be removed before sticking the pickups to the soundboard.

7.4 Stick the pickups onto the inside of the lid. The lid is the soundboard.

Be aware of the need to open the lid for maintenance so place the pickups where there is sufficient length of wire for the lid to open easily and not pull the wires.

Chapter 8

Attaching the machine heads

8.1 Secure the guitar carefully protecting the varnish!

Note that the guitar neck has been secured but the finish has been protected by foam kneeling pads.

8.2

Drill a very small hole for each machine head screw.

(Some machine heads *need two screws)*

8.3 The screws must be very small so that they do not poke through the other side.

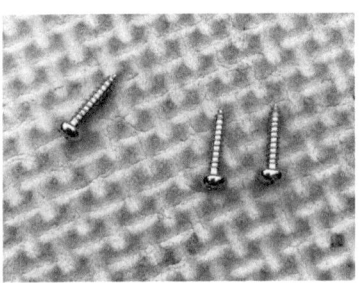

8.4 Screw the machine heads in place

Chapter 9

Stringing the Guitar

9.1 Because this version of a slide guitar is acoustic with piezo-electric pickups it is possible to use any type of string. However we have found that the best strings in practice are phosphor bronze acoustic guitar strings. They sound the least scratchy when the slide is moved over them but are strong and also usable with electromagnetic pickups.

Here is an example of a pack of strings purchased online:

9.2 For this guitar we chose the three thickest strings, the 6,5 and 4. These are the bottom E, the A and D strings. Various other combinations can be used....again it is a matter of preference.

9.3 Put the two bridges ready so that you can place them in their respective sites, the bolt in the groove near the machine heads and the box bridge on the place chosen for it on the cigar box.

9.4 Thread the first string through the tail end and pull it up to the machine head. At this point the bridges are not in place but as you tighten the string you put them in place. They do not need to be stuck in, the tension will keep them in place.

Golden Rule : It is important to make sure that the string winds in such a way that the end that goes along the guitar does not ride up but goes downwards on the post of the machine head. If it winds upwards it is likely to jump off the top when you play the guitar.

9.5 The ends of the strings are rather long so snip them off

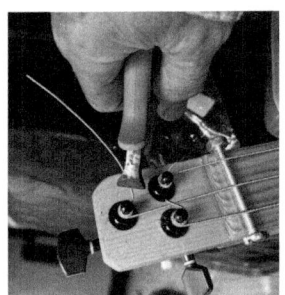

9.6 Tune the guitar using an electronic tuner. These can be purchased online for a few pounds: search for "clip-on guitar tuner."

The three string slide guitars are usually tuned to an open chord known as a "power chord". In this case we tuned the bottom string to E, the middle to B and the top to an E above the bottom string.

Golden Rule : Tune up rather than down.

Chapter 10

Playing the guitar

10.1 The guitar is played using a guitar slide. Historically they were made from the necks of glass bottles, hence the name "bottleneck guitar." Now slides are made from glass, plastic, metal or porcelain. They can be purchased online relatively cheaply. Search for "guitar slide".

10.2 The slide is placed on either the middle or ring finger of the left hand. Keep the slide as close to parallel with the fret line as possible. To do this slacken the grip of your left hand and just touch the strings. You do not need to push very hard and certainly do not try to push the strings down onto the fretboard.

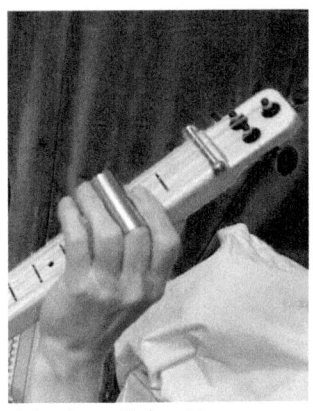

Golden Rule : Touch the strings with the slide. Do not push down onto the fretboard.

10.3 Amplification: when playing the guitar at a gig a big amplifier may be needed but for practice and busking a small battery driven amplifier is probably sufficient. These can be purchased online and are made by companies as prestigious as Marshall. The amplifier will clip into your belt and you can then play the guitar wherever you like! (Within reason!) They have a socket for headphones.

Above: Very small amplifiers measuring about 11cm x 11cm x 6cm.

Below: Short lead with ¼ inch jack plugs at both ends.

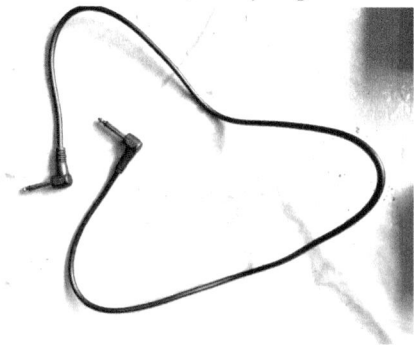

You will need a lead. These can be purchased online. The sockets on the pickups and amplifier are for 1/4 inch (or 6.3mm) jack plugs.

10.4 Guitar picks (also known as plectrums) are triangular shaped plastic pieces used to pick at the guitar strings. They come in various sizes and rigidity.

And (almost) Finally:

Golden Rule : Enjoy playing your guitar!

Social media

Do search for me on Youtube, Facebook and Instagram: look for Paul R Goddard: you'll recognise me from the cover photo for this book.

Good luck and good playing!

Dr Jazz Slide Guitars are on sale at **Hobgoblin Music** stores around the UK and online https://hobgoblin.com. Also stocked at **Clevedon Music Shop**. I will occasionally put guitars at special sale prices on my social media. My email address is **paulrgoddard@me.com**

Appendix

Fret Spacings for various scale lengths

The fret scale is measured bridge to bridge: machine head bridge (MHB) to box bridge. The starred* frets are the octaves

580mm fret scale

Fret	From MHB in mm
1	32.6mm
2	63.3
3	92.3
4	119.7
5	145.5
6	169.9
7	192.9
8	214.6
9	235.1
10	254.5
11	272.8
12*	290
13	306.3
14	321.6
15	336.1
16	349.8
17	362.7
18	374.9
19	386.4
20	397.3

600mm fret scale

Fret	From MHB in mm
1	33.7mm
2	65.5
3	95.5
4	123.8
5	150.5
6	175.7
7	199.5
8	222
9	243.2
10	263.3
11	282.1
12*	300
13	316.8
14	332.7
15	347.7
16	361.9
17	375.3
18	387.9
19	399.8
20	411

640mm fret scale

Fret	From MHB in mm
1	35.9mm
2	69.8
3	101.8
4	132
5	160.5
6	187.5
7	212.9
8	236.8
9	259.5
10	280.8
11	301
12*	320
13	338
14	354.9
15	370.9
16	386
17	400.3
18	413.7
19	426.4
20	438.4
21	449.7
22	460.4
23	470.5
24**	480

680mm fret scale

Fret	From MHB in mm
1	38.2mm
2	74.2
3	108.2
4	140.3
5	170.6
6	199.2
7	226.2
8	251.6
9	275.7
10	298.4
11	319.8
12*	340
13	359.1
14	377.1
15	394.1
16	410.1
17	425.3
18	439.6
19	453.1
20	465.8
21	477.8
22	489.2
23	499.9
24**	510

Octaves are starred *